MYTHOLOGY
AROUND THE WORLD

ROMAN
MYTHS

by Eric Braun

Consultant:
Laurel Bowman, PhD
Assistant Professor and Graduate Advisor
Greek and Roman Studies
University of Victoria

CAPSTONE PRESS
a capstone imprint

Fact Finders Books are published by Capstone Press,
1710 Roe Crest Drive, North Mankato, Minnesota 56003
www.mycapstone.com

Library of Congress Cataloging-in-Publication Data
Names: Braun, Eric, 1971– author.
Title: Roman Myths / by Eric Braun.
Description: North Mankato: Capstone Press, 2019. |
Series: Fact Finders: Mythology Around the World
Identifiers: LCCN 2018010995 (print) | LCCN 2018020439 (ebook) |
ISBN 9781515796053 (library binding) | ISBN 9781515796190 (paperback) |
ISBN 9781515796121 (eBook PDF)
Subjects: LCSH: Mythology, Roman—Juvenile literature.
Classification: LCC BL803 .B73 2018 (print) | LCC BL803 (ebook) | DDC 292.1/3—dc23
LC record available at https://lccn.loc.gov/2018010995

Editorial Credits
Editor: Jennifer Huston
Production Artist: Kazuko Collins
Designer: Russell Griesmer
Media Researcher: Morgan Walters
Production specialist: Kathy McColley

Photo Credits: Alamy: Chronicle, 19, Florilegius, 13, Peter Horree, 24; Bridgeman Images: Morgan,
Evelyn De (1855–1919)/De Morgan Collection, courtesy of the De Morgan Foundation, 21; Getty
Images: Culture Club, 9, 20, 23, De Agostini/Biblioteca Ambrosiana, 26, Kean Collection, 17, Nastasic,
27, Photo Josse/Leemage, 8; iStockphoto: duncan1890, 6; Newscom: Active Museum/Le Pictorium,
5, akg-images, 25, Ken Welsh, 11, Liszt Collection, 22; North Wind Picture Archives, 4; Shutterstock:
G.roman, (lightning) 1, cover, LALS STOCK, 29, Lukasz Szwaj, (paper texture) design element
throughout, Madredus, (grunge) design element throughout, MatiasDelCarmine, 14, 15, Peter
Hermes Furian, 7, photocell, (plate) design element throughout, RaZZeRs, (flare) 1, cover, Steinar, top
middle, 15, T.SALAMATIK, (rain texture) design element throughout, vukkostic91, Cover

Printed and bound in the USA.
PA021

TABLE OF CONTENTS

CHAPTER 1

THE CULTURE OF ANCIENT ROME

When you think of ancient Rome, do you picture beautiful marble buildings and statues? Or maybe you think of clashing swords and **gladiator** fights. You may have heard stories of powerful emperors and giant armies.

But before all that, Rome was nothing more than a small settlement on a hill. According to some stories, Rome was founded in 753 BC by Romulus and Remus. They were the twin sons of Mars, the god of war. Romulus killed Remus and became the first king of Rome, which is named for him.

Many gladiator fights took place in the Colosseum, a stadium in ancient Rome.

The growing city was ruled by kings until 509 BC. After that Rome became a **republic**—meaning it was governed by the people. Instead of kings who ruled for life, Rome had elected officials who served for a set number of years. Rome's first laws were carved on 12 bronze tablets known as the Twelve Tables. They were displayed in the **Roman Forum** in 450 BC.

PALATINE HILL

Palatine Hill was in the center of Rome. It is said that Rome was founded on the hill. Later it became the area where emperors and other wealthy Romans lived in huge, beautiful homes. The word *palace* comes from Palatine Hill.

gladiator—a man in ancient Rome who fought other men or wild animals, often to the death, to provide entertainment

republic—a government where the people elect a small group of people to make decisions for the whole; also the word for a country with that kind of government

Roman Forum—the town square in Rome where ancient government buildings stood, and where the ruins of many buildings still stand

Rome grew quickly in size and power. By the early 3rd century BC, the Romans ruled all of Italy. By AD 117 they ruled everything around the Mediterranean Sea. The Roman Empire went as far north as present-day Great Britain and as far south as parts of Africa. But as Rome grew, it became harder to govern the massive territory. The gap between rich and poor widened, and military leaders began to battle for power. One of those military

leaders was Julius Caesar, a general with great success expanding Rome's territory. Caesar became the ruler of Rome in 45 BC after his army won a civil war in Italy. When Caesar took power, it began a period of several hundred years when Rome was ruled by emperors.

Julius Caesar was one of the greatest rulers of ancient Rome.

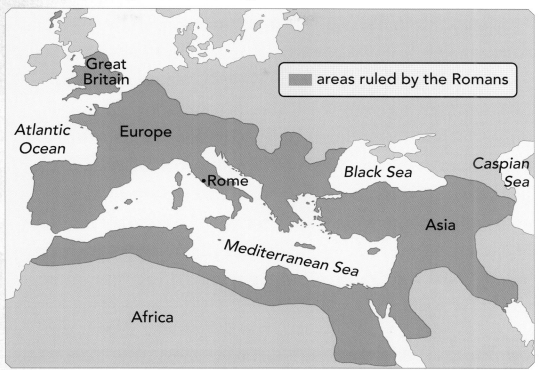

Great Britain

Atlantic Ocean

Europe

areas ruled by the Romans

•Rome

Black Sea

Caspian Sea

Asia

Mediterranean Sea

Africa

RICH AND POOR

Life in ancient Rome could be very different depending on one's social class. Wealthy Romans lived in nice homes outside the noisy, dirty city. They had servants and slaves and lived grand lifestyles. But most Romans were poor. They lived in small, cramped homes in the city and worked hard just to survive. They attended chariot races and gladiator fights.

Rich or poor, many parts of Roman life were the same for all families. Only men were the heads of households and could own property. Women were expected to take care of the home and the children.

Adopted Cultures

Ancient Romans were strongly **influenced** by the other **cultures** that Rome traded with and conquered. They were particularly influenced by the Greeks, whom they had conquered in 146 BC. The Romans soon adopted the art, philosophy, and literature of the Greeks. The earliest Latin **epic poem** discovered was a translation of a Greek work, *The Odyssey* by Homer. Over time, other classic Greek plays and poems were translated into Latin, the language of ancient Rome. Roman poets and playwrights, including Virgil, Ovid, and Horace, soon began writing their own works as well.

Virgil (left) relates one of his poems before Horace (center) and two statesmen.

A heartbroken Dido cries out as her beloved Aeneas sails away in Virgil's *Aeneid*.

Many of the early works the Romans created were based on stories from other cultures. Virgil based his epic poem *The Aeneid* on the Trojan hero Aeneas, who originally appeared in *The Iliad* by Homer.

DID YOU KNOW?

An emperor rules an entire empire, which is made up of several countries or territories. A king typically rules over just one country.

influence—to have an effect on someone or something

culture—a group of people's beliefs, customs, and way of life

epic poem—a long story or poem about heroic adventures and great battles

Roman Religion

The Romans worshipped the same gods as the Greeks, but they gave them different names. The Romans retold many of the Greek myths, using the gods' Roman names. Like the Greeks, the Romans believed that some of these tales contained factual, historical information.

In some ways Roman religion was different from Greek religion. For the Greeks, religion was a public activity. Romans worshipped mainly in the home. Most public religious ceremonies and festivals were for the head of the family only. It was typically the husband who performed religious **rituals** for the family. He also communicated with spirits in order to protect his family.

ritual—an action that is always performed in the same way, usually as part of a religious or social ceremony

sacrifice—to offer something to a god

The Romans believed the gods controlled everything that happened on Earth and were actively involved in their daily lives. They thought that bad things would happen if the gods became angry or unhappy with them. The Romans felt they earned the gods' approval by properly observing religious rituals. For example, it was tradition in Rome to set a place and serve food at each meal for a god or spirit. They also might offer food or an animal **sacrifice** in exchange for favors.

In this Roman ritual, a bull, a sheep, and a pig are given as an offering to the god Mars in hopes that he will bless the land.

CHAPTER 2

THE ROMAN GODS AND GODDESSES

Romans had myths about how the world began. The most common of these myths said the world began in darkness called Chaos. Chaos contained everything that would ever exist, but it was all disorganized. Then the first four forces began to take shape. The first of these was Cupid, the mighty force of love. Then came Terra, the Earth. Next was Tartarus, the Underworld, and finally Nox, or night.

Caelus, who was the sky, came later. He and Terra gave birth to the Titans, the first **immortal** beings. One of these Titans was Saturn, who ruled the world. Saturn and his wife, Ops, were the parents of the first gods—Jupiter, Juno, Neptune, Vesta, Ceres, and Pluto.

In addition to worshipping gods, the Romans also honored spirits. Spirits protected the family, home, and even trees, rivers, fields, and buildings. The spirits worshipped in the home were unique to each family. Every family had special shrines in the home to worship them. The head of the household made sacrifices to the spirits to make sure they would continue to watch over the family.

immortal—able to live forever

Chaos (left) in human form, and Ops, the Great Mother of all Roman gods

ROMAN GODS AND GODDESSES

Everyone in ancient Rome worshipped the same gods and goddesses. The main Roman gods and goddesses were adapted from those of the ancient Greeks. Each had special skills or powers and ruled a certain part of life.

SATURN

JUNO was the queen of the gods and the protector of Rome. She was the goddess of motherhood and childbearing.

JUPITER was the ruler of the Roman gods. As the god of the sky, Jupiter was often pictured throwing a lightning bolt. To the ancient Romans, thunder and lightning occurred when Jupiter was angry.

PLUTO was the ruler of the Underworld and the god of the dead.

VULCAN was a son of Juno and Jupiter. As the god of fire, he was associated with craftsmanship and metalworking.

MARS, another son of Jupiter and Juno, was the god of spring, agriculture, anger, revenge, courage, fertility, and war.

MINERVA, Jupiter's daughter, was the goddess of wisdom, learning, the arts, sciences, medicine, crafts, and war.

NEPTUNE was the god of the sea. Neptune's most important symbol was the trident—the three-pronged spear that he carried.

VESTA was the goddess of the home, family, and hearth. She was one of the most-worshipped gods in ancient Rome.

CERES was a goddess of agriculture, grain, fertility, and motherhood. She was honored at marriages, funerals, and harvest time.

APOLLO was the god of music and healing, and he was said to have taught humans medicine. As the god of light, he was in charge of driving the sun across the sky every day with his golden chariot.

DIANA, the goddess of the moon, nature, and hunting, was usually shown with a hunting dog and a bow and arrow.

VENUS was the goddess of love and beauty, as well as spring, gardens, and vineyards.

MERCURY was a messenger for the gods, so he had winged sandals to help him get around quickly.

CHAPTER 3

THE STORIES

Inspired by the Greek myths, the Romans retold the stories in Latin with their own gods substituted for the Greek ones. Roman audiences loved the tales, which were full of drama and mystery.

MINERVA AND ARACHNE

One myth tells the story of Arachne, a girl who boasted that she could weave more beautifully than the goddess Minerva. This angered Minerva, so she challenged Arachne to a weaving contest. The two sat at their looms to work.

Minerva's beautiful **tapestry** showed herself winning the weaving contest and humans being punished for challenging the gods. Arachne's tapestry showed scenes of the gods tricking mortals. Minerva realized that Arachne's tapestry was gorgeous, but she declared herself the winner. Then she turned Arachne into a spider, making her destined to weave webs forever.

tapestry—a heavy piece of cloth with threads woven into it to make pictures or patterns

Unhappy with Arachne's tapestry, Minerva turned her into a spider.

PLUTO AND PROSERPINA

To the ancient Romans, the myth of Pluto and Proserpina helped them understand the changing of the seasons. One day Proserpina, the daughter of Ceres, was picking flowers in a field. Pluto saw Proserpina and immediately fell in love with her. He took her back to the Underworld as his wife.

Overwhelmed with grief, Ceres searched the world looking for her daughter. She even journeyed to the Underworld. But when she tried to rescue her daughter, Pluto would not give her up. While away from her daughter, Ceres had neglected the earth's crops. People were dying for lack of food. Jupiter stepped in and ordered Pluto to give Proserpina back to her mother.

But before she returned, Proserpina ate some seeds she had found in the Underworld. It was decided that because she had eaten in the Underworld, she must remain there. However, Jupiter ruled that Proserpina could go back to her mother. But she had to return to Pluto and the Underworld for several months each year. The ancient Romans believed spring and summer represented the months of the year that Proserpina spent with her mother. Fall and winter occurred when she was forced to return to Pluto and the Underworld.

Pluto took Proserpina to live with him in the Underworld.

A Long Journey and a Date with Fate

One of the most important stories traced the origin of Rome back to the Trojan War. The Trojan War was a major battle between the Greeks and the people of Troy (Trojans). Virgil's epic poem *The Aeneid* follows the Trojan hero Aeneas, who first appeared in the Greek classic *The Iliad*. Like the Greek tales, Roman stories featured the gods living among humans and influencing important events.

After the Greeks destroyed Troy during the war, Aeneas escaped the city with the help of his mother, Venus. While at sea, Aeneas and his men were caught in a terrible storm. They were also chased by harpies, eaglelike creatures with women's faces. It was the first of many misadventures that would keep the sailors traveling for years.

In Virgil's *Aeneid*, Juno whipped up a storm to throw Aeneas' ship off course.

APOLLO AND CASSANDRA

In one ancient myth, Apollo visited one of his temples in Troy. There he saw a beautiful young Trojan priestess named Cassandra.

Apollo fell in love with Cassandra and offered her a gift. In exchange for her love, he would give her the ability to see the future. Cassandra agreed. But as soon as she did, she saw that Apollo would help the Greeks defeat Troy in the Trojan War. This upset Cassandra, and she refused to be with Apollo, which made him very angry.

Apollo could not take back the gift, so instead, he made it so that nobody would ever believe Cassandra's **prophecies**. Toward the end of the Trojan War, Greek soldiers hid inside a giant wooden horse, waiting to be taken inside the walls of Troy. Cassandra predicted that it was a trick and that Troy would fall. But when she tried to warn the Trojans, nobody believed her.

prophecy—a prediction

On one of his stops, Aeneas learned that his fate was to establish a great city in Italy. Aeneas spoke with an **oracle** who took him on a trip to the Underworld. While there, he saw his dead father, who told him more about his fate. Aeneas' father told him that his **descendants** would eventually establish a great city and powerful nation. That was why it was so important for Aeneas to reach Italy. So that is where he headed.

With the help of an oracle, Aeneas journeyed through the Underworld to speak with his father.

The giant Cyclopes tried to kill Aeneas and his men.

On the way, Aeneas and his men confronted the Cyclopes, a group of one-eyed giants who attacked them. They escaped, but Juno caused Aeneas to face many trials on his journey. Juno hated the Trojans, particularly Aeneas because she knew that his descendants would one day conquer her favorite city, Carthage.

oracle—a place or person that a god speaks through; in myths, gods used oracles to predict the future or to tell people how to solve problems

descendants—all the relatives who trace their family roots back to one person

Finally Aeneas arrived in Italy at a place called Latium that was ruled by King Latinus. The king had a beautiful daughter named Lavinia. Latinus agreed to let Lavinia marry Aeneas. But his wife, Queen Amata, wanted their daughter to marry a powerful warrior named Turnus. Turnus put together an army to destroy Aeneas and the Trojans. In response, Aeneas gathered allies from neighboring nations, and a brutal war broke out. Aeneas' army won the war, and he married Princess Lavinia. He then built a city and named it Lavinium.

When Aeneas arrived in Latium, he met with King Latinus.

ROMULUS AND REMUS

Romulus and Remus were the twin sons of the god Mars. Their mother was the daughter of King Numitor, whose family tree could be traced all the way back to Aeneas. When Romulus and Remus were infants, their grandfather Numitor was defeated by his younger brother Amulius and lost control of his kingdom. Amulius ordered a servant to drown Romulus and Remus in the river. He knew the boys would be heirs to the throne, and he wanted to preserve his power.

When Romulus and Remus were babies, their uncle ordered them drowned to prevent them from taking power as adults.

But the servant felt sorry for the boys and placed them in a basket on the river instead. The basket floated down the river where a wolf found the twins and took care of them. Eventually a herdsman raised the boys, and they grew up to be strong and brave. When Romulus and Remus were older, they killed Amulius and put Numitor back on the throne.

After finding Romulus and Remus floating on the river, a herdsman took the boys home.

The brothers then decided to build a new city. But they argued and fought over the city's location. Ultimately, Romulus killed Remus and named the new town Rome after himself. According to this story, Rome was founded on the day Remus died—April 21, 753 BC. Rome would eventually become the most powerful nation

According to legend, Romulus and Remus, were the founders of Rome.

in the world at the time. Through this complicated story, the Romans traced their existence and power to the gods.

DID YOU KNOW?

Romulus was said to have made Rome a safe place for people running away from slavery. Rome also welcomed others from neighboring areas who wanted to make a fresh start.

CHAPTER 4

THE END OF THE ANCIENT ROMAN RELIGION

As the Roman Empire grew, the influence of the myths grew weaker. Roman writers changed the stories when they wanted to rather than carrying on the traditional versions.

At the same time, other religions began to gain followers. One of these religions was Christianity. Unlike traditional Roman religion, Christians worshipped only one god. Their rituals were also very different from those of the traditional Roman religion. Because of this, Christians in the Roman Empire were sometimes arrested, tortured, and killed for their beliefs.

THE SPLIT OF THE EMPIRE AND THE RISE OF CHRISTIANITY

During his time as emperor (AD 379–392), Theodosius I worked hard to stamp out the traditional Roman religion and spread Christianity. He made Christianity the official religion of the Roman Empire in AD 380.

In 395 the Roman Empire was split in two. The Eastern Empire became the Byzantine Empire. It lasted until 1453. But the Western Roman Empire declined. In AD 476 a soldier named Odovacar overthrew the last Roman emperor and became king of Italy.

The Roman Empire was gone. But the Roman gods and goddesses and their myths continue to live on in poetry, literature, art, and architecture.

THE HAGIA SOPHIA

The Hagia Sophia in Istanbul, Turkey, is the best-known Christian church from the Byzantine Empire. It was completed in 537 for emperor Justinian I. Despite several earthquakes and a fire, the building still stands nearly 1,500 years later.

Glossary

culture (KUHL-chur)—a group of people's beliefs, customs, and way of life

descendants (di-SEN-duhnts)—all the relatives who trace their family roots back to one person

epic poem (EP-ik POH-uhm)—a long story or poem about heroic adventures and great battles

gladiator (GLAD-ee-ay-tur)—a man in ancient Rome who fought other men or wild animals, often to the death, to provide entertainment

immortal (i-MOR-tuhl)—able to live forever

influence (IN-floo-uhnss)—to have an effect on someone or something

oracle (OR-uh-kuhl)—a place or person that a god speaks through; in myths, gods used oracles to predict the future or to tell people how to solve problems

prophecy (PRAH-fuh-see)—a prediction

republic (ri-PUHB-lik)—a government where the people elect a small group of people to make decisions for the whole; also the word for a country with that kind of government

ritual (RICH-oo-uhl)—an action that is always performed in the same way, usually as part of a religious or social ceremony

Roman Forum (ROH-muhn FOR-uhm)—the town square in Rome where ancient government buildings stood, and where the ruins of many buildings still stand

sacrifice (SAK-ruh-fise)—to offer something to a god

tapestry (TAP-i-stree)—a heavy piece of cloth with threads woven into it to make pictures or patterns

READ MORE

James, Simon. *Ancient Rome.* Eyewitness Books. New York: DK Children, 2015.

Mincks, Margaret. *What We Get from Roman Mythology.* Mythology and Culture. Ann Arbor, Mich.: Cherry Lake Publishing, 2015.

Wolfson, Evelyn. *Mythology of the Romans.* Mythology, Myths, and Legends. Berkeley Heights, N.J.: Enslow Publishers, 2014.

INTERNET SITES

Use FactHound to find Internet sites related to this book.

Visit www.facthound.com

Just type in 9781515796053 and go.

 Check out projects, games and lots more at
www.capstonekids.com

CRITICAL THINKING QUESTIONS

1. The Romans adopted the cultures of other nations. Name some aspects of your country's culture that have come from other nations.

2. The Roman myths often had gods interacting with humans. They also frequently involved themes of jealousy, anger, or love. Reread one of the Roman myths in this book, and discuss the motivation for the god's or goddess' actions.

3. Make up your own gods and goddesses. What special traits or powers do they have? What part of life do they control. Write a myth about them.

INDEX